BIANCA GIBSON

ON PURPOSE

ALLOW YOURSELF TO RELEASE, REPLENISH, RECHARGE AND RESET

Paperback ISBN: 978-1-63616-194-5
eBook ISBN: 978-1-63616-195-2

Published By Opportune Independent Publishing Co.
www.opportunepublishing.com

Printed in the United States of America

For permission requests, please email the publisher with the subject line as "Attention: Permissions Coordinator" to the email address below:

Info@Opportunepublishing.com

CONTENTS

PRINCIPLE ONE: **Thought-Provoking Genre**

Let's carefully consider how we think. Sometimes, the way in which we think can cause confusion, set unrealistic expectations, and create chaos within our minds. Let's practice creating a healthy mental living space in our minds by becoming self-aware.

- Defining Self-awareness
- MIND Phase
- Cognitive Restructuring
- Short Stories
- Dr. Seuss Quotes/Reflection
- Poetry

PRINCIPLE TWO: **Wellness**

Let's get into what it means to take care of both physical and mental health: the act of practicing healthy habits daily to attain better physical and mental health outcomes so that instead of surviving, you're thriving.

- Define Balance
- BODY Phase
- Societal (Social) Roles
- Short Stories
- Dr. Seuss Quotes/Reflection
- Poetry

PRINCIPLE THREE: **Soul Consciousness**

Let's explore what it feels like to know the power, beauty, and identity of who we are to the core, focusing on the common originality of all beautiful things.

- Define Choice
- SPIRIT Phase
- Holistic Mindset
- Short Stories
- Dr. Seuss Quotes/Reflection
- Poetry

DO YOU

Hey there, friend! I hope this message reaches you well. By the time you're at the end of this book, your ship will be ready to sail. Cast your net in all the open waters. Trust your instincts, pace yourself, and be unbothered. GO, FRIEND, GO! See, I'm already on your team. Close your eyes, but don't you dare dream! Be open to adventurous voyages, embarkments, and all things new. Most of all, my friend, DO YOU!

—B. Gibson

PRINCIPLE ONE

Thought-Provoking Genre

WORD OF THE DAY:

1. **Self-awareness:** Conscious knowledge of one's own character, feelings, motives, and desires.
2. **Mind Phase** ◯ A circle is defined as a round-shaped figure that has no corners or edges.

One might wonder, *What does a shape have to do with my mind or the way in which I think?* Think about the saying, "Don't box yourself in." What do you think this means? I believe it means, do not allow yourself restrictions of things or people that you believe are challenging to accomplish or obtain. The circle is a metaphorical representation of the ideal resemblance of our mind and brain, hence round; all senses are derived from within and full, without edges or corners. The functioning of the brain consists of receiving information from our five senses, which are sight, smell, sound, touch, and taste. Our brain also receives other input, such as touch, vibrations, pain, and temperature. The brain functions in the capacity that enables us to experience a plethora of things, such as "thoughts and decisions, memories, emotions, movement, balance and coordination, automatic behavior such as breathing, heart rate, sleep and temperature control, fight or flight response (stress response), perception of various sensations including pain, speech and language functions, and regulation of organ function.

- A few things to ponder are as follows: When the brain has obtained an enormous amount of information, is it possible to consider information overload? When, and if, this happens, were there a combination of factors, such as people, environment, scents, and/or survival tactics involved that influenced decision-making? Were there certain feelings and emotions felt that were provocative, which resulted in an unforeseen outcome? What happens when the brain has reached its capacity of thoughts, circumstances, and situations? Does the functioning of the brain continue to produce healthy thoughts after enduring lack of aesthetic thoughts?

If you'd respond in logic, it is appropriate to believe that all the ponders above are considerably possible to acknowledge that as a result in the incapability of a healthy brain functioning within reason and logic, one will not demonstrate intriguing behaviors due to associated stressors.

PAUSE ON PURPOSE

Take a five-minute break before you continue your reading experience—allow yourself to take three deep breaths while focusing on your breathing.

During this break, I hope that you've allowed yourself to just relax. Remember, we don't always have to be getting things done. This pause was very intentional for you to allow your brain a rest after taking in education on the topic of discussion. I hope that you will learn to incorporate Pause on Purpose in your daily life.

- **Cognitive Restructuring:** A technique that has been successfully used to help people change the way they think. The goal consists of replacing stress-producing thoughts with more balanced thoughts that do not produce stress. (i.e., person feels anxious about a break-in taking place in their home; emotional reasoning would tell them that this is because A break-in is likely to happen.)
- Challenging negative thoughts; replace negative thinking with positive thinking.
  1. *Negative thought*: "I will never experience genuine love." Positive thought: "I am going to allow myself to meet someone nice and see what happens."
  2. *Negative thought*: "I can't afford to start a business when I'm only making a little money. Positive thought "I'm not making the kind of money that I desire. However, I will start saving a little at a time to start my business."
  3. *Negative thought*: "Life is depressing, and I will never get over this depression." Positive thought: "I know that things are challenging right now, but I also know that I can feel better."

FIRST SHORT STORY:

Bianca's Story

On July 25, 2021, I experienced HELL! I was hospitalized due to my inability to breathe properly on my own. Needless to say, I needed an oxygen concentrator provided by the hospital, as I also learned that I tested positive for COVID-19 as well as pneumonia. To say that I was sadly astonished would be an understatement; I was horrified! Fast forward, after learning that my liver, lungs, and heart were not functioning properly and independently, I received oxygen daily, multiple CAT scans, high blood pressure medication (diagnosis of hypertension), diagnosis of anxiety, blood drawn twice a day, two daily injections of steroids in my stomach, and continuous negative reports from the doctors and nurses. Oh, I was doomed for sure! I died mentally, emotionally, and spiritually, and my body was shutting down just as I allowed these negative forces to impede my mental space.

Around my ninth day of being in the hospital, I made up my mind and decided that I was going to LIVE and not die! I started to walk on my own and shower. I opened the blinds in my room, although the view overlooked the building of the hospital—but it was sunny most days, and I wanted to see that, even if I couldn't feel it. Long story short, when I had finally decided to stop feeling sorry for myself and self-sabotaging, EVERYTHING started to get better; the test results were improving, my breathing was getting better, and I didn't need the oxygen all day. I was moving around after days of lying in the hospital bed and only getting up to use the restroom and wash myself. I lost weight, which I could stand to lose, thankfully. I discharged myself on day 16, and today, I am mentally, spiritually, physically, and emotionally healthier than I have ever been in my entire life.

Yes, I still have some complications lingering; however, there isn't anything that I will allow to consume my thoughts in a negative way. I changed my mind, and it changed my life!

—Bianca G.

SECOND SHORT STORY:

Bianca's Experience

One day, while working with my 13-year-old client that has a diagnosis of major depressive disorder, I proposed this "Would You Rather" questionnaire: "Would you rather be a mannequin or a tree?"

I continued to say, "A tree has roots, a past, a possible future, and with water and sun, it grows. Meanwhile, a mannequin is simply a display that has no ability to move, to speak, to live—it can just be."

Working in the field of mental health can be very challenging, even after 20 years in different arenas. This question allowed my client to think in depth about what she wanted for her life while giving perspective to the metaphorical representation of a tree and a mannequin. I'm happy that my client chose to be a tree.

—Bianca G.

QUOTE Corner

"Today, you are you! That is truer than true! There is no one alive that is you-er than you!"

— Dr. Seuss

PAUSE ON PURPOSE REFLECTION:

Catchphrase is "a word or expression that is used repeatedly and conveniently to represent or characterize a person, group, idea, or point of view. This quote allows one to focus on true self and identity." After reading this quote as many times as you'd like, pause and reflect on who you are and if you are your true self.

"The more that you read, the more things you will know. The more that you learn, the more places you'll go."

— Dr. Seuss

PAUSE ON PURPOSE REFLECTION:

Education is "the act or process of things or acquiring general knowledge, developing the powers of reasoning and judgment, and generally of preparing oneself or others intellectually for mature life." Reading is fundamental. We not only gain knowledge but we allow our brains to acquire information that can be beneficial in many ways as we travel through life.

POETRY

A Traveler's Mind

If I stretch my wings to fly really, really, really high, would I be so high that I'm amongst the clouds, stars, and the sun? I wonder, if I allowed myself to go far and wide, that not only would I become an explorer but even a smooth and free glide—a glide that guides and that leads people far beyond their own beliefs and imaginations. I bet that when people undercover their own abilities, they would know for sure just how far they can go, and that will be their confirmation. Affirmations, unspoken truths, and deep—really deep—power of words will search and find their lips to speak aloud, and very proud to know, to feel, and to just be. Oh, but how evident would it be if we allowed ourselves to travel this world not only in the physical aspect but allowing ourselves to believe, receive, achieve, and to be appeased by our own ability to just be.

See, a voyager is willing to travel without limits and free from unrealistic expectations but arrives to many destinations. Imaginations are only as real as we allow them to be, to see, and to leave a place with peace of mind. Gentle and kind, we define those characteristics to fit what we have encountered with others and wonders of how great things can get when we allow ourselves to just forget. Forget the norm and the typical things in life, sacrifice, and just go within these times. Oh, how far you can go when you unlock a traveler's mind.

—Bianca G.

Deep and Wide, Side to Side

When we've searched high and low, up and down, all around, deep and wide, side to side, have we discovered anything that requires us to think, feel, or believe that there's more to experience and desire while we're alive?

What have we discovered, if anything at all? Are we able to amaze ourselves while we take time to pause? During this time of stillness, sit in the emotion of just being present and doing nothing, nothing at all. Relax in your freedom to do nothing but pause.

We're searching high and low, up and down, all around, deep and wide, side to side. Now that you've experienced what it's like to think, feel, and believe, you've given yourself permission to not only be in it but to be more present than you've ever tried.

Now, go in peace, my friend; go on about your journey. Release, replenish, recharge, and reset. Live life on your own terms and absent of regret. Acknowledge but don't be moved by fear or pain; charge it to the game. Rename, demolish any signs of defame, rename, regain, manifest your strength and dignity to move in confidence and pride. You've now accomplished what you once searched for high and low, up and down, all around, deep and wide, side to side.

—Bianca G.

PAUSE

18

MIND

Mental Capacity

Mental Space

Mentality

Thoughts

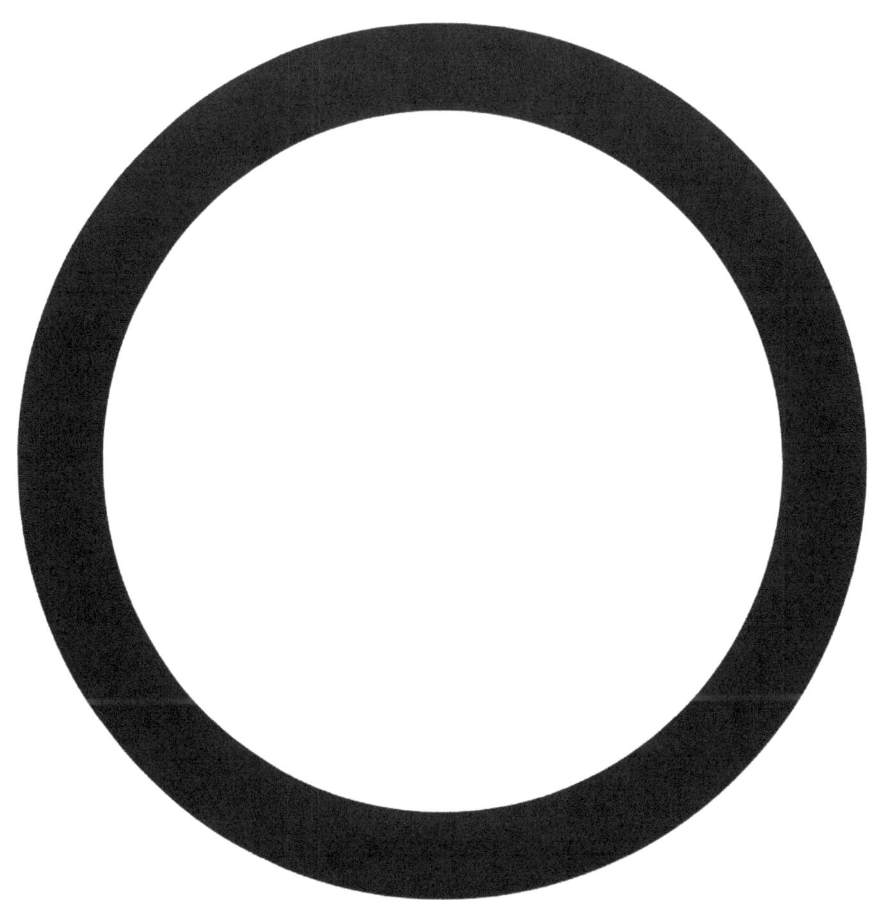

PRINCIPLE TWO

Wellness

WORD OF THE DAY:

1. **Balance:** An even distribution of weight enabling someone or something to remain upright and steady.
2. **BODY Phase:** △ A triangle shape is defined as plane figure with three straight sides and three angles.

Imagine being on a camping trip, and you have a toolbox full of all the things you believe you'd need if an unforeseen situation were to arise. In this toolbox, you have a flashlight, a first aid kit, scissors, rope, toilet paper, a tent, a sleeping bag, a map, and even a backup flashlight. One would probably think that they're prepared for the woods.

All these items mentioned are essentials; however, water and food would help the camper to get a lot further with nutrients and hydration. Being in the wilderness can be alarming in the event of coming across an aggressive bear, poisonous snake, or even a wrong turn to take you off your path. It must be considered that the body will start to experience extreme conditions after going so long without food and water; therefore, it would be wise to consider packing at least a couple of water bottles and snacks. Although it has yet to be determined how long a human can go without food, it has been said that a person can survive between eight and 21 days without food.

However, after about two weeks, "as the breakdown of muscle speeds up, the body begins to lose heart, kidney, and liver function"—things considered if a person is presumed healthy. So, imagine if there's a host and/or illness living inside the body that has yet to be confirmed, and a person goes without food and water sources as the body starts to respond to the unknown illness.

- A few things to ponder are as follows: When thinking in the obvious mind, it is the semantics we consider, such as survival tactics; however, we can also think in the logic mind, hence to thrive, which allows us to think of longevity and prosperity of this life and not the quick fix that doesn't grant us long-lasting fulfillment of good health and strength.

PAUSE ON PURPOSE

Take a five-minute break before you continue your reading experience. Grab a coffee or tea, or just relax. During this break, I hope that you've allowed yourself to just relax. Remember, we don't always have to be getting things done. This pause was very intentional for you to allow your brain a rest after taking in education on the topic of discussion. I hope that you will learn to incorporate Pause on Purpose in your daily life.

1. **Societal (Social) Role** (Perceived Pressures): A socially defined pattern of behavior that is expected of persons who occupy a certain social position or belong to a particular social category.

   Society impacts our decision-making about work, school, relationships, and life in general. One can say that society doesn't impact their life negatively or positively; however, there's no medium—either we will or will not do things, say things, and think. However, if we are not capable of doing any of these things, one must consider the possibility of inability pertaining to physical, mental, and emotional disadvantages.

   - Your mind has three states: "The reasonable mind, the emotional mind, and the wise mind. While everyone possesses each of these states, it has been said that people usually gravitate toward a specific one most of the time."

1. <u>**The Emotional Mind**</u>: Is used when feelings control a person's thoughts and behavior. They might act impulsively with little regard for consequences. *Ex. A person quits their job due to their supervisor giving them a verbal warning for three consecutive late arrivals to work.*

2. <u>**The Wise Mind**</u>: Refers to a balance between the reasonable and

emotional halves. They can recognize and respect their feelings while responding to them in a rational manner. *Example: Accepting a higher paying job in another city or state while simultaneously considering the cost of relocating and distance between family and friends along with the advanced opportunities and potential growth with a thriving organization.*

3. <u>**A Reasonable Mind**</u>: A person uses their reasonable mind when they approach a situation intellectually. They plan and make decisions based on fact. *Example: Returning to school to study business management while occupying a position that requires educational advancement for promotion to a managerial position with pay increases.*

FIRST SHORT STORY:

Tejpal's Story

For a couple of years, I was involved in road bike racing. My very specific training program included workouts focusing on a particular cadence, power output, and heart rate. Par of this program was a recovery ride, an interval during which the biker backs off speed and power output while the cadence remains high. During these intervals, I decided to monitor my heart rate and compare it to the thoughts and emotions I was experiencing. When I was visualizing myself winning the next race—and without pedaling harder—my heart rate would go up to 30 beats more per minute. My mental and emotional body affected my physical body.

SECOND SHORT STORY:

Carrol's Story

In December of 2008, I was overwhelmed, depressed, and worried about my daughter. My whole being was calling out for me to dig out of my malaise, but I didn't seem able to start the journey back to contentment.

I had heard of an inspirational life coach named Joe Vitale. Excited at the idea of having some help and guidance, I contacted his team and learned that he was offering a series of personal coaching sessions. Then, I found out that the price tag for this coaching series was $5,000, an amount that was absolutely impossible for me at that time.

Discouraged, I tried to remain open to possibilities, and, on a whim, I stopped in to check my mailbox at the University of Arizona, even though we were on Christmas break and there was no reason for me to go there. Inside my mailbox was a solitary envelope, and I opened it with curiosity. In it, I found a check for $10,000. It was from a supporter who had come to many of my concerts but whom I did not personally know. All the note said was, "I believe in what you are doing, and this money is to support whatever you need it for."

This generous gift allowed me to work extensively with a life coach, which not only reframed my emotions and my sense of contentment but also allowed me to manifest and publish my first book, *Power Performance*. I shifted from a place of feeling powerless to being excited about my own potential, and this newfound enthusiasm extended beyond me personally, subsequently inspiring thousands of musicians around the world to believe in themselves and claim their excellence."

QUOTE Corner

"If things start happening, don't worry, don't stew. Just go right along, and you'll start happening, too."

— Dr. Seuss

PAUSE ON PURPOSE REFLECTION:

Hyper-focused: Highly focused attention that lasts a long time (i.e., you concentrate so hard that you lose focus on everything else around you.).

We experience life from different dimensions, whether that be specific focus on family, friends, acquaintances, lovers, coworkers, strangers, and other groups. One who is fixated on a person and/or thing, may wrap their thoughts, feelings, emotions, and reality around these things and somehow lose themselves in the mix.

Pause and allow yourself to reflect on your life and whether you are immersed in another person and/or thing. If you find that you are, seek clarity of what causes you to lose sight of self, and start working on refocusing your mind to concentrate on YOU.

"Think left and think right and think low and think high. Oh, the thinks you can think up if only you try!"

— Dr. Seuss

PAUSE ON PURPOSE REFLECTION:

Vortex: You have an attitude of "All is well"; you experience emotions on the high end of the emotional scale, like appreciation, love, and happiness. Being in a vortex is high vibe; it's a positively aligned state of being. You are satisfied with what is, and you are eager for more.

Experiencing a spiritual vortex can be both liberating and demanding. Life seems to take us on journeys that our conscious mind hasn't prepared for but our unconscious mind experiences. Thus, the spiritual vortex is extremely powerful and can enhance meditation, self-discovery, and spiritual growth;

however, one must be able to experience being free from doubt and open to the journey of a new and profound commitment to self-indulging enlightenment. **Pause** and allow yourself to make a conscious decision regarding where you are in your vortex and if your current state of mind is going to help you to advance to the next level or keep you stagnant.

POETRY

Freestyle

As open, as up and down, as free as can be; as alongside and as behind, as not yet true, as I believe. As focused, as content as my mind can be. As above, so below; as shadowed, as fast, as possible, and as far as I can see. As what I feel, and as what I know to be. As happy, as free, as wise as I choose to be. As I recall, as I know, as I think, and so it is that I believe. As reasonable, as achievable, as unbeknownst to me. As I travel along my journey, as free and lively as I can be. As I plant my seed, as I watch it grow, as beautiful as it is to me. As my life is truly remarkable as it can be, as strong and withstanding, as big, as tall, as free as I can be. As loving, as caring, as busy as I can be. As slow, as understanding, as far, as wide, as far as I choose to see. As the distance I choose to travel matters, as every inch, as every kilometer, as each millimeter, as so every mile.

As I am as far as I choose to be, as every path, as every road, I've chosen to take the route that says, *Welcome to be as free*, as free, as free, as freestyle as I desire to be.

—Bianca G.

The Cause

It is said that often in this life, there are causes and effects of everything that we do and even what we believe. Small possibilities, big dreams, slow talk, fast pace—what does this really mean? Reassured yet tackled by the overwhelming doubt and disbeliefs, grief, despair, trouble in paradise, love, loyalty, and all the other things that we believe. No one chooses to just *be*. And then, one begins to wonder, *What in the world did I do?* or *Where did I go wrong?* Often, we forget to pause, and we dare not to take time to be alone.

Let's get into the real stuff and not push aside what needs to be said and what needs to be done. Let us remember the importance of peace, solitude, and the light which refocuses the sun. The cause is that which we have chosen to act upon, and it is what it will be, while the effect of many things in this life is the result of what we choose not to see. Let us not confuse opportunity with choice, as we can choose to release, replenish, recharge, and reset just for YOU!

—Bianca G.

PAUSE

31

BODY

Perception

Wellness

Resilience

Survival

PRINCIPLE THREE

Soul Consciousness

WORD OF THE DAY:

1. **Choice:** An act of selecting or making a decision when faced with two or more possibilities.

2. **Spirit Phase:** ☐ A square is defined as a quadrilateral with all four angles right angles and all four sides of the same length. So, a square is a special kind of rectangle; it is one where all the sides have the same length. Thus, every square is a rectangle because it is a quadrilateral with all four angles right angles.

As you've read earlier in one of the poems, as above so below, which simply means, "What happens in a higher realm or plane of existence also happens in a lower realm." Inside of this spiritual realm, you have the power to create your own reality. In doing so, get into the vortex of tuning in to who you are. ☞ Connect with your spiritual guide, and allow yourself to be in a vibrational alignment. One may ask, *How do I connect with my spirit self?* I'm glad you asked! First, you must be intentional and vigilant about what you want and what you desire. Get yourself in a place of nonresistance; this means to not doubt. You must position your mind in a quiet space to be free from negative energies, including your own. Per Abraham Hicks, "The process of meditation allows one to quiet the mind. In this process, you stop thoughts, and when you stop thoughts, you stop resistance, and when you stop resistant thoughts, then your vibration raises, and you can begin to hear." I'd only add to tap into journaling and writing to allow yourself the freedom of tending to your vibration. As you write, you will begin to create and/or recreate source energy. Source energy promotes wealth, health, and alignment as you're in the process of experiencing joy, and you're elated by the freedom of just floating in your vortex.

3. **Holistic Mindset:** Addressing the whole person—mind, body, and spirit. What we believe, what we think, and what we do, whether being aesthetically on purpose, we are allowed to think, feel, and be what we so desire. There's a holistic approach that provides support to this theory and looks at the whole person—their physical, emotional, social, and spiritual well-being. To identify seven aspects of holistic health, we must think beyond the physical health and be mindful of the interconnected aspects: the physical, mental, social, emotional, intellectual, vocational, and environmental health.

   1. **The physical wellness**—getting enough rest, eating well, drinking enough water, and moving our body.

   2. **The mental wellness**—challenge the brain, pursue hard things, and choose brain-boosting food.

   3. **The social wellness**—set healthy boundaries, spend time with family and friends, and connect with the outside world.

   4. **The emotional wellness**—journal, write, talk to someone, and practice mindfulness and meditation.

   5. **The spiritual wellness**—enjoy time in nature, indulge in relaxation, and take time to do deep breathing and grounding exercises.

   6. **The vocational wellness**—follow your passion, and do the things that make you feel good and alive.

   7. **The environmental wellness**—create sustainable habits, become more educated on healthy environmental products and use them, garden, and indulge in natural environment surroundings.

- A few things to ponder are as follows: You don't have to be ready; you just have to start. There are so many things that have been accomplished in life by people, including myself, who were not ready; however, we started, we endured, we experienced, and, therefore, we have done. The spiritual power of manifestation is connected to your soul—your soul is the core of your being, your essence. Manifest moment to moment. *8 Principles* (1. You have a unique soul mission; 2. It's all about energy; 3. Intuition is the magic wand; 4. Your belief and your story do not define you and can be changed; 5. Your desire forms the basis of every manifestation; 6. Intention overcomes every obstacle; 7. You have the power to clear, heal, and reinvent constantly; and 8. Your inner guidance knows the path to creating life balance) *to Create the Life You Truly Desire* by Tejpal and Dr. Carrol McLaughlin offers a wealthy perspective on life and how to apply principles to a profound spiritual journey led and guided by oneself.

PAUSE ON PURPOSE

Take a five-minute break before you continue your reading experience. *Wheeew*, that was a lot, huh? Very good stuff, though. Abraham Hicks, along with other spiritually and emotionally intelligent beings, have created powerful resources for people like you me to receive. I am enjoying writing this book because I'm learning as I go, as well. Ever felt like you just have so much on your brain, and the only way to get it out is to write it down? Yep—me, too!

Many nights while sleeping (well, I thought I was sleeping), I'd jump up and head to my office/closet and jot something down on a random sheet of paper because I knew that I would use it one day. Today, as you're reading this material, I can almost promise you that thoughts popped into my brain in the wee hours, and you're reading the subconscious, wired up brain that put this entire book into context to help guide and encourage your life's journey. STAY TUNED . . . I have so much more subconscious stuff to share.

FIRST SHORT STORY:

Tejpal's Story

"My parents always believed that the world was not a welcoming place and that every aspect of existence had to be challenging and hard. It took me years to realize that I was also carrying this belief. I was always guarded and vigilant yet disconnected from my feelings and the amount of fear I was experiencing. When I started working, I was always attracted to the most difficult assignments that had a high level of risk.

With the help of counselors and healers, I discovered that I was holding my parents' beliefs and realized that I didn't have to hang on to them. I started to trust the world more, learned to ask for help, and attracted situations that were more in alignment with my soul mission. From being a driven, demanding leader always asking for more, I was able to develop my ability to listen and receive to help people around the world enhance their lives."

SECOND SHORT STORY:

Carrol's Story

"I was having the worst time trying to clear the clutter of papers on my desk, though I really wanted it to be done. I would pick up a piece of paper and then put it down because I was indecisive about what to do with it. I would pick up another piece of paper, maybe a bill, and remember that I needed to call the company to check if it was accurate or not. But that involved finding some other papers (Agh!), so I'd put that paper back down.

I was in a spin. Every time I was unable to complete a necessary step, I slid further down into the vortex of unfulfilled energy. Accompanying this terrifying dive was self-recrimination ("I should have done that weeks ago!"), emotional fatigue, and finally paralysis.

Remembering that the antidote for the spin is action, I decided to choose just one piece of paper and take action on it. At the bottom of the pile, I found a phone number related to a (by now outdated) request for a musician, and I telephoned the agency. I was surprised when the woman I spoke with offered me a new opportunity to perform and for much more money! Not only did a nice new opportunity arise, but I was also astounded at how little time this simple action took. Refreshed and enthused, I was confident to take more steps and not be trapped in the energy tornado I had experienced so often. As the 'spin' energy cleared, a variety of new possibilities opened up."

QUOTE Corner

"You'll be on your way up! You'll be seeing great sights! You'll join the highfliers who soar to high heights."

— Dr. Seuss

PAUSE ON PURPOSE REFLECTION:

Mind capacity—Your ability to understand information and make decisions about your life.

During times of perplexity, we can allow ourselves time to release, replenish, recharge, and reset as much as we need to. Our minds can and will allow only so much information before we become overwhelmed with our own thoughts. It is imperative that we choose to utilize breaks to pause and do nothing.

"You're off to great places! Today is your day! Your mountain is waiting. SO . . . get on your way!"

— Dr. Seuss

PAUSE ON PURPOSE REFLECTION:

Emanate—Release, cast, expel, emit (i.e., to be mesmerized by the love and wisdom that emanated from him).

Another word that comes to mind when thinking of emanate is evolve. To evolve, we must allow ourselves time and space to grow, and sometimes, growth comes from uncomfortableness. During this stage of quietness and stillness, we, too, are experiencing a reality that is immersive yet steadfast and conscious.

POETRY

Freedom

Whatsoever it is that one desires, believes, and creates will be their reality and truth. Whenever or wherever one chooses to be, to see, to feel, and to live is, too, what they will ultimately do. REALITY is what it is and so to be. REALITY is a belief yet current stance in what we desire, aspire to, and set forth, our own empire through our visual lenses of what we will see. For those things that we wish to accomplish and obtain, be vigilant, be bold, be precise, be disciplined, and just be.

Look around you, beside you—more so, focus on what lies ahead, for your past is behind you; therefore, all things made new will also be free. Be powerful, but don't force anything that doesn't fit in the spaces you've made fillable, available, not wasteful but sacred and open to fine choices and great selections as you so desire to experience in this life. Make wise decisions; be slow to answer, quick to think but not too fast to speak yet make room for all the things that are soul-felt beautifully and all that feels right. What is to be, what it is, and what's before you are what will come. Clear the path for all things made new, made whole, and jovial in your soul, and prepare for what you've created, which is indescribable yet close in reach: FREEDOM.

—Bianca G.

PAUSE

42

SPIRIT

Wholeness
Freedom
Choice
Desire

44

ABOUT THE AUTHOR

Bianca Cheney-Gibson, often known as B, is a resident of The Woodlands, a suburban area near Houston, Texas, though her roots trace back to Georgia. Born in Macon and primarily raised between Macon and Atlanta, she maintains strong ties with her family and friends in the region.

As a mother and a proud GiGi to her cherished grandson, Jasiah, Bianca's heart is firmly invested in her family. Her interests encompass an array of activities, including travel, reading, writing, pool, and engaging in spirited debates. With a remarkable travel history that includes over 20 countries and counting, she finds the world an endless source of inspiration.

An avid reader, Bianca enjoys a diverse range of novel genres, from drama and fantasy to mystery and horror, with a particular fondness for inspirational, spiritual, and motivational literature. Her career in the mental health field spans over two decades, where she has made a significant impact. As a certified life coach, she continues to be a beacon of support and guidance to those she serves.

Bianca's love for music is as eclectic as her interests, spanning R&B, hip-hop, pop, rock, jazz, country, electronic, reggae, disco, and more. She revels in the thrill of live performances and a wide array of musical genres. However, her true passion lies in writing. Since the age of 10, when she received her first typewriter, she has been captivated by the written word. Her journey as a writer began with poetry, often freestyled in the moment.

In her book, readers will discover her creatively composed poetry, reflecting her love for themes such as love, adventure, spirituality, and life. With thoughtfulness and personal reflection, Bianca has crafted this book to provide readers with a meaningful guide to "Pause on Purpose," drawing from her life experiences and wisdom. Though she aspires to engage in open mic or spoken word performances, she has also been an appreciative audience member, applauding the talents of fellow artists.

Through her writing and shared experiences, Bianca Cheney-Gibson hopes to inspire and guide others on their own journeys of self-discovery and purposeful reflection.

Love,
B

ALL YOU

Little, big, or small, take breaks through it ALL.

Laugh out loud, and you can even shout. Forgive yourself, reflect, and air things out.

Make plans, follow them through, and if it doesn't work out, still choose YOU.

Give yourself grace. Even when you feel like you've failed, you haven't. Be calm, gentle, and kind, as your ship will sail.

Lastly, my friend, don't forget to smile, and stand up tall in everything you do. Remember, this is ALL YOU.

—B.Gibson

48